Low-Carb, High-Taste

A recipe book for Carb-Conscious Cooking

Ashley Anderson

Table of the Contents

Introduction

Welcome to our weight-loss recipe book! In this collection, we've curated a variety of delicious and healthy meals that will not only help you lose weight but also help you maintain a healthy weight in the long run. Our recipes are designed to be low in calories, high in nutrients, and easy to make. We've made sure to include a wide range of dishes, from breakfast to dinner, so you'll never get bored of eating the same thing. With our recipes, you'll be able to enjoy tasty meals while still reaching your weight-loss goals. So, whether you're looking to lose a few pounds or just maintain a healthy weight, this recipe book is for you. Let's get started!

Appetizers

Caprese Skewers

Ingredients:

- 1 pint cherry tomatoes
- 8 oz fresh mozzarella cheese, cut into small cubes
- 1/4 cup fresh basil leaves
- 2 tbsp olive oil
- Salt and pepper, to taste

Instructions:

1. Thread cherry tomatoes and mozzarella cubes onto skewers, alternating between the two.
2. In a small bowl, mix together olive oil, salt, and pepper.
3. Brush skewers with the oil mixture, then place them on a preheated grill. Grill for 3-4 minutes on each side, or until the cheese is slightly melted and the tomatoes are slightly charred.

4. Remove skewers from the grill and place them on a serving platter.

5. Garnish skewers with fresh basil leaves.

6. Serve immediately and enjoy!

This recipe is a healthy and delicious appetizer that is low in calories and high in flavor. The fresh mozzarella and cherry tomatoes are a classic combination that is sure to please any crowd.

Cucumber and Feta Bites

Ingredients:

- 1 large cucumber
- 1/2 cup crumbled feta cheese
- 1/4 cup chopped fresh mint
- 1 tablespoon lemon juice
- 1 teaspoon olive oil
- Salt and pepper to taste

Instructions:

1. Slice the cucumber into 1/4 inch rounds.

2. In a small bowl, mix together the feta, mint, lemon juice, olive oil, and salt and pepper.

3. Top each cucumber round with a small spoonful of the feta mixture.

4. Serve immediately and enjoy!

Note: You can also add some chopped tomatoes for a different flavor.

Spinach and Ricotta Stuffed Mushrooms

Ingredients:

- 8 medium-sized mushrooms
- 1 cup fresh spinach leaves, chopped
- 1/4 cup ricotta cheese
- 1/4 cup grated Parmesan cheese
- 1 clove of garlic, minced
- 1 tablespoon breadcrumbs
- Salt and pepper to taste

Instructions:

1. Preheat the oven to 350°F (175°C).
2. Remove the stems from the mushrooms and chop them finely.
3. In a pan, sauté the mushroom stems, garlic, and spinach until the spinach is wilted.
4. Remove from heat and let it cool.
5. In a bowl, mix the ricotta, Parmesan, sautéed mixture, breadcrumbs and seasoning.
6. Stuff the mixture into the mushroom caps.
7. Arrange the mushrooms on a baking sheet and bake for about 20 minutes.
8. Remove from the oven and let them cool for a few minutes before serving.

Enjoy!

Deviled Eggs

Ingredients:

- 6 large eggs

- 2 tablespoons mayonnaise

- 1 teaspoon Dijon mustard

- 1 teaspoon honey

- Salt and pepper to taste

- Paprika for garnish

Instructions:

1. Place the eggs in a saucepan and cover with water. Bring to a boil, then reduce the heat and simmer for 9 minutes.

2. Remove the eggs from the heat and place them in a bowl of ice water for 5 minutes.

3. Peel the eggs and cut them in half lengthwise. Remove the yolks and place them in a separate bowl.

4. Mash the yolks with a fork, then add the mayonnaise, Dijon mustard, honey, salt, and pepper. Mix until smooth.

5. Spoon the mixture into the egg whites.

6. Garnish with paprika and chill in the refrigerator for 30 minutes before serving.

Enjoy!

Vegetable Crudites with Yogurt Dip

Ingredients:

- Assorted vegetables such as carrots, celery, cucumber, bell peppers, and broccoli florets
- 1/2 cup plain Greek yogurt
- 1 clove of garlic, minced
- 1 tablespoon lemon juice
- Salt and pepper to taste

Instructions:

1. Cut the vegetables into bite-size pieces and arrange them on a platter.
2. In a small mixing bowl, whisk together the yogurt, garlic, lemon juice, salt and pepper until combined.
3. Serve the yogurt dip alongside the vegetable crudités.

You can also add some herbs such as dill or parsley to the dip to make it more flavorful. This is a great way to enjoy a variety of fresh vegetables while keeping the calorie count low.

Enjoy!

Baked Zucchini Fries

Ingredients:

- 2 medium zucchinis
- 1/4 cup all-purpose flour
- 1/4 cup grated Parmesan cheese
- 1/4 teaspoon garlic powder
- Salt and pepper to taste
- 1 egg
- 1/2 cup panko breadcrumbs

Instructions:

1. Preheat the oven to 425°F (220°C).
2. Cut the zucchinis into thin, french fry-shaped slices.
3. In a shallow dish, mix together the flour, Parmesan, garlic powder, salt and pepper.
4. In a separate shallow dish, beat the egg.
5. In a third shallow dish, add the panko breadcrumbs.
6. Dip each zucchini slice in the flour mixture, then the egg mixture, and finally the breadcrumbs.

7. Place the zucchini slices on a baking sheet lined with parchment paper.

8. Bake for 15-20 minutes, or until golden brown and crispy.

9. Serve immediately and enjoy!

You can also use different herbs and spices to make the fries have different flavor like cayenne, cumin, or dried herbs.

Cucumber and Tomato Salad

Ingredients:

- 1 medium cucumber, thinly sliced
- 1 medium tomato, diced
- 1/4 cup diced red onion
- 2 tablespoons chopped fresh parsley
- 1 tablespoon olive oil
- 1 tablespoon red wine vinegar
- Salt and pepper to taste

Instructions:

1. In a large bowl, combine the cucumber, tomato, red onion, and parsley.
2. In a small bowl, whisk together the olive oil, red wine vinegar, salt and pepper.
3. Pour the dressing over the vegetables and toss to combine.
4. Let the salad sit for at least 15 minutes, or until the vegetables have released some of their juices.
5. Serve the salad chilled or at room temperature.

You can add some feta cheese or olives for more flavor and different texture. This is a refreshing and healthy appetizer that is perfect for summertime.

Enjoy!

Spinach and Feta Stuffed Mushrooms

Ingredients:

- 8 large mushrooms
- 1/4 cup chopped onion
- 1 cloves garlic, minced
- 2 cups spinach leaves, chopped
- 1/4 cup crumbled feta cheese
- 1/4 cup plain breadcrumbs
- 1/4 cup grated Parmesan cheese
- 1 tablespoon olive oil
- Salt and pepper to taste

Instructions:

1. Preheat the oven to 350°F (175°C).
2. Clean the mushrooms by gently wiping them with a damp cloth. Remove the stems and chop them.
3. In a pan over medium heat, add olive oil and sauté the chopped mushroom stems, onion, and garlic until softened.
4. Add the spinach leaves and cook until wilted.

5. Remove from heat and stir in feta cheese, breadcrumbs, Parmesan cheese, and season with salt and pepper.

6. Using a spoon, stuff the mushroom caps with the spinach mixture.

7. Place the mushrooms on a baking sheet lined with parchment paper.

8. Bake for 20-25 minutes or until the mushrooms are tender and the filling is golden brown.

9. Serve warm and enjoy!

This recipe is a great way to enjoy the taste of mushrooms while keeping the calorie count low.

Grilled Eggplant Rolls

Ingredients:

- 1 large eggplant, sliced into 1/4-inch rounds
- 1 cup ricotta cheese
- 1/4 cup grated Parmesan cheese
- 2 cloves garlic, minced
- 2 tablespoons chopped fresh basil

- 1/4 teaspoon salt

- 1/4 teaspoon black pepper

- 1/2 cup marinara sauce

Instructions:

1. Preheat the grill to medium-high heat.

2. In a small bowl, mix together the ricotta cheese, Parmesan cheese, garlic, basil, salt and pepper.

3. Spread a spoonful of the cheese mixture onto each eggplant slice.

4. Roll the eggplant slices and secure with toothpicks.

5. Grill the eggplant rolls for about 5 minutes per side or until the eggplant is tender.

6. Serve the eggplant rolls with the marinara sauce on the side for dipping.

This recipe is a great way to enjoy eggplant with a flavorful and healthy twist.

Zucchini and Carrot Fritters

Ingredients:

- 1 medium zucchini, grated
- 2 medium carrots, grated
- 1/4 cup all-purpose flour
- 1 egg
- 1/4 cup diced onion
- 2 cloves of garlic, minced
- 2 tablespoons chopped fresh parsley
- Salt and pepper to taste
- Olive oil for frying

Instructions:

1. In a large bowl, mix together the grated zucchini, grated carrots, flour, egg, onion, garlic, parsley, salt and pepper.
2. Heat a skillet over medium heat and add enough oil to coat the bottom of the pan.
3. Use a spoon to drop the batter by tablespoons into the hot oil.

4. Fry the fritters for 2-3 minutes per side or until golden brown.

5. Drain the fritters on a paper towel-lined plate.

6. Serve the fritters warm with your favorite dipping sauce.

This recipe is a great way to enjoy the taste of zucchini and carrot while keeping the calorie count low.

Cucumber and Dill Yogurt Dip

Ingredients:

- 1 cup plain Greek yogurt
- 1/2 of a cucumber, finely diced
- 1 tablespoon chopped fresh dill
- 1 clove of garlic, minced
- 1/4 teaspoon salt
- 1/4 teaspoon black pepper
- Crudités such as carrots, celery, bell peppers, and cucumber for dipping

Instructions:

1. In a medium bowl, mix together the Greek yogurt, diced cucumber, dill, garlic, salt, and pepper.
2. Cover and refrigerate for at least 30 minutes to allow the flavors to meld together.
3. Serve the dip with crudités for dipping.

This recipe is a great way to enjoy a creamy and flavorful dip without the added calories. Greek yogurt is a great source of protein and the cucumber and dill give it a refreshing taste.

Spinach and Artichoke Stuffed Mushroom

Ingredients:

- 12 large mushrooms
- 1 cup fresh spinach, chopped
- 1/2 cup canned artichoke hearts, chopped
- 1/4 cup grated Parmesan cheese
- 2 cloves garlic, minced
- 2 tablespoons chopped fresh parsley
- Salt and pepper to taste

Instructions:

1. Preheat the oven to 375°F (190°C).
2. Remove the stems from the mushrooms and chop them finely.
3. In a large bowl, mix together the chopped mushroom stems, spinach, artichoke hearts, Parmesan cheese, garlic, parsley, salt, and pepper.
4. Stuff the mushroom caps with the mixture.
5. Place the mushrooms on a baking sheet and bake for 20-25 minutes or until the mushrooms are tender and the tops are golden brown.
6. Serve warm.

This recipe is a great way to enjoy the taste of spinach and artichoke while keeping the calorie count low. These mushrooms are low in calorie, but packed with flavor and nutrients.

Zucchini and Feta Rolls

Ingredients:

- 2 medium zucchinis
- 1/4 cup crumbled feta cheese
- 1/4 cup chopped fresh mint
- 2 cloves of garlic, minced
- Salt and pepper to taste
- Olive oil for brushing

Instructions:

1. Preheat the oven to 375°F (190°C).
2. Using a mandoline or a sharp knife, slice the zucchinis lengthwise into thin strips.
3. In a small bowl, mix together the feta cheese, mint, garlic, salt, and pepper.
4. Place a spoonful of the feta mixture on one end of each zucchini strip and roll it up.
5. Brush the rolls with olive oil and place them on a baking sheet.
6. Bake for 15-20 minutes or until the zucchini is tender and the feta is melted.

7. Serve warm.

This recipe is a great way to enjoy the taste of feta and mint while keeping the calorie count low. These zucchini rolls are low in calorie, but packed with flavor and nutrients.

Cucumber and Smoked Salmon Rolls

Ingredients:

- 1 large cucumber
- 4 oz of smoked salmon
- 2 tbsp of Cream cheese
- 1 tbsp of chopped fresh dill
- Salt and pepper to taste

Instructions:

1. Cut the cucumber into slices about 1/4 inch thick.
2. Mix cream cheese, dill, salt, and pepper in a small bowl.
3. Spread cream cheese mixture on each cucumber slice.
4. Place a small piece of smoked salmon on top of each cucumber slice

5. Roll the cucumber slice and press gently to seal.

6. Refrigerate for at least 30 minutes before serving.

This recipe is a great way to enjoy the taste of smoked salmon and dill while keeping the calorie count low. These cucumber rolls are low in calorie, but packed with flavor and nutrients.

Tomato and Mozzarella Skewers

Ingredients:

- 1 pint cherry tomatoes
- 8 oz fresh mozzarella balls
- 1/4 cup chopped fresh basil
- 2 cloves of garlic, minced
- 1/4 cup balsamic vinegar
- Salt and pepper to taste
- Skewers

Instructions:

1. Preheat the grill or grill pan to medium-high heat.

2. Thread cherry tomatoes and mozzarella balls onto skewers, alternating between the two.
3. In a small bowl, mix together the basil, garlic, balsamic vinegar, salt, and pepper.
4. Brush the skewers with the balsamic mixture.
5. Grill the skewers for 2-3 minutes per side or until the tomatoes are slightly charred and the mozzarella is melted.
6. Serve warm.

This recipe is a great way to enjoy the taste of fresh tomatoes and mozzarella while keeping the calorie count low. These skewers are low in calorie, but packed with flavor and nutrients.

Zucchini Carpaccio

Ingredients:

- 2 medium zucchinis
- 2 tbsp of lemon juice
- 2 tbsp of olive oil
- 1/4 tsp of salt

- 1/4 tsp of black pepper

- 2 tbsp of grated parmesan cheese

- 2 tbsp of chopped fresh basil

Instructions:

1. Using a mandoline or a sharp knife, slice the zucchinis into very thin rounds.

2. In a small bowl, whisk together the lemon juice, olive oil, salt, and pepper.

3. Arrange the zucchini slices on a platter or on individual plates.

4. Drizzle the lemon dressing over the zucchini.

5. Sprinkle grated parmesan cheese and chopped basil over the top.

6. Serve chilled or at room temperature.

This recipe is a great way to enjoy the taste of fresh zucchinis while keeping the calorie count low. It is a light and refreshing dish that is perfect for a summer appetizer.

Cucumber and Greek Yogurt Dip

Ingredients:

- 1 large cucumber, peeled and finely diced
- 1 cup plain Greek yogurt
- 1/4 cup chopped fresh dill
- 1 tbsp fresh lemon juice
- 1 clove of garlic, minced
- Salt and pepper to taste
- Crackers or veggies for dipping

Instructions:

1. In a medium bowl, combine the diced cucumber, Greek yogurt, dill, lemon juice, garlic, salt, and pepper.
2. Mix well until all ingredients are evenly combined.
3. Cover and refrigerate for at least 30 minutes to allow flavors to meld.
4. Serve the dip with crackers or veggies for dipping.

This recipe is a great way to enjoy the taste of fresh cucumber and Greek yogurt while keeping the calorie count low. The dip is low in calorie, but packed with flavor and nutrients. It's a great option for a healthy appetizer or snack.

Tomato and Mozzarella

Ingredients:

- 10 cherry tomatoes
- 10 small mozzarella balls (bocconcini)
- 10 basil leaves
- 1 tbsp olive oil
- Salt and pepper to taste

Instructions:

1. On each skewer, thread a cherry tomato, a mozzarella ball, and a basil leaf. Repeat until the skewer is full.
2. In a small bowl, mix together the olive oil, salt, and pepper.
3. Brush the skewers with the olive oil mixture.
4. Heat grill or grill pan over medium-high heat. Grill the skewers for 2-3 minutes per side or until tomatoes are slightly charred and the mozzarella is melted.

5. Serve the skewers warm and enjoy!

This recipe is a great way to enjoy the taste of fresh tomatoes, mozzarella, and basil while keeping the calorie count low. It's a simple, yet delicious appetizer that can be prepared in minutes. The skewers can be prepared on the grill or in a grill pan, making it a perfect summer appetizer.

Cucumber and Yogurt Dip

Ingredients:

- 1 English cucumber, peeled and grated
- 1 cup plain Greek yogurt
- 2 cloves garlic, minced
- 1 tbsp lemon juice
- 1 tsp dill, chopped
- Salt and pepper to taste

Instructions:

1. In a fine mesh strainer, place the grated cucumber and press down to remove excess water.

2. In a mixing bowl, combine the yogurt, garlic, lemon juice, dill, salt and pepper.

3. Stir in the squeezed cucumber.

4. Cover and refrigerate for at least 30 minutes to allow the flavors to meld.

5. Serve the dip chilled with veggies or pita chips.

This recipe is a great way to enjoy the taste of fresh cucumber and yogurt while keeping the calorie count low. It's a simple, yet delicious appetizer that can be prepared in minutes. The dip can be served with vegetables or pita chips, making it a perfect summer appetizer.

Tomato and Basil Bruschetta

Ingredients:

- 4 slices of whole grain bread
- 1 large tomato, diced
- 2 cloves of garlic, minced
- 2 tbsp fresh basil, chopped
- 1 tbsp olive oil

- Salt and pepper to taste

Instructions:

1. Preheat the oven to 350°F (175°C).
2. Place the bread slices on a baking sheet and drizzle with olive oil.
3. Bake for 5-7 minutes or until lightly toasted.
4. In a mixing bowl, combine the diced tomato, minced garlic, chopped basil, salt, and pepper.
5. Once the bread is toasted, remove it from the oven and rub the top of each slice with a clove of garlic.
6. Top each slice of bread with the tomato mixture.
7. Place the bruschetta back into the oven and bake for an additional 5-7 minutes or until the tomatoes are slightly softened.
8. Remove from the oven and serve hot.

This recipe is a great way to enjoy the taste of fresh tomatoes and basil while keeping the calorie count low. It's a simple, yet delicious appetizer that can be prepared in minutes. The bruschetta can be served hot and is perfect for a light summer appetizer.

Cucumber and Feta Dip

Ingredients:

- 1 large cucumber, peeled and diced
- 1 cup of crumbled feta cheese
- 1/4 cup of plain Greek yogurt
- 2 cloves of garlic, minced
- 2 tbsp fresh dill, chopped
- Salt and pepper to taste

Instructions:

1. In a mixing bowl, combine the diced cucumber, crumbled feta cheese, Greek yogurt, minced garlic, chopped dill, salt, and pepper.
2. Mix well until all the ingredients are well combined.
3. Taste and adjust seasoning as needed.
4. Cover and refrigerate for at least 30 minutes before serving to allow the flavors to meld together.
5. Serve with whole grain crackers or vegetables such as cucumber slices or bell pepper strips.

This recipe is a delicious and healthy appetizer option that is perfect for a summer gathering. The cool cucumber and tangy feta cheese are a great combination, while the yogurt and garlic add a creamy and flavorful touch. It's a low-calorie appetizer that is easy to make and is sure to be a hit with your guests.

Breakfast

Berry and Yogurt Parfait

Ingredients:

- 1 cup of mixed berries (strawberries, blueberries, raspberries)
- 1 cup of low-fat Greek yogurt
- 1/4 cup of rolled oats
- 1 tbsp honey
- 1 tsp of vanilla extract

Instructions:

1. In a small mixing bowl, combine the rolled oats, honey, and vanilla extract. Mix well.
2. In a clear glass or parfait dish, layer the mixed berries, yogurt, and oat mixture.
3. Repeat the layering process until all ingredients are used.
4. Serve immediately or store in the refrigerator for up to 2 days.
5. Enjoy your delicious and healthy breakfast parfait.

This recipe is a delicious and healthy option for breakfast. The mixed berries add natural sweetness and a burst of flavor, while the Greek yogurt provides protein and the oats add a nice crunch. The honey and vanilla extract bring out the natural sweetness of the berries and yogurt. You can customize the recipe by using your favorite berries, or adding some nuts or seeds for added crunch. This recipe is easy to make and is perfect for a low-calorie breakfast that will keep you full and satisfied until lunchtime.

Breakfast Smoothie Recipe

Ingredients:

- 1 cup frozen berries (strawberries, blueberries, raspberries, etc.)
- 1 banana
- 1/2 cup plain Greek yogurt
- 1/2 cup almond milk
- 1 tsp honey (optional)

Instructions:

1. Add all ingredients to a blender.
2. Blend until smooth and creamy.
3. Pour into a glass and enjoy!

This smoothie is a great way to start your day because it's packed with nutrients, antioxidants, and protein. Berries are low in calories but high in vitamins and antioxidants. Greek yogurt provides protein to keep you full and banana adds a creamy texture and natural sweetness. Almond milk is lower in calories than cow's milk, but still provides a good source of calcium. Add honey for a little extra sweetness if desired. This smoothie is also very versatile, you can replace the berries with any other fruits you prefer.

Breakfast Parfait Recipe

Ingredients:

- 1 cup low-fat Greek yogurt
- 1/2 cup mixed berries (strawberries, blueberries, raspberries)

- 1/4 cup granola (homemade or store-bought)

Instructions:

1. In a small bowl or jar, layer 1/4 cup of Greek yogurt.
2. Add 1/4 cup of mixed berries on top of the yogurt.
3. Sprinkle 1 tablespoon of granola on top of the berries.
4. Repeat the layering process one more time, ending with granola on top.
5. Enjoy your parfait chilled.

This low-calorie breakfast parfait is a delicious and nutritious way to start your day. Greek yogurt is high in protein, which will keep you full and satisfied until lunchtime. Berries provide antioxidants and are low in calories. Granola gives it a nice crunch and added flavor. You can swap the berries with any other fruits you prefer or add some nuts or seeds for added texture and flavor. This parfait is perfect for busy mornings, you can make it the night before and grab it on your way out.

Breakfast Smoothie Bowl

Ingredients:

- 1 banana
- 1/2 cup frozen berries (strawberries, blueberries, raspberries)
- 1/2 cup Greek yogurt
- 1/4 cup rolled oats
- 1/4 cup almond milk
- 1 tsp honey (optional)

Instructions:

1. In a blender, combine the banana, frozen berries, Greek yogurt, rolled oats, and almond milk. Blend until smooth.
2. If desired, add honey for sweetness.
3. Pour the smoothie mixture into a bowl and top with your favorite toppings, such as berries, nuts, or granola.
4. Enjoy your delicious and healthy breakfast smoothie bowl!

Note: You can use any frozen fruit you like and also you can add protein powder if you want.

Breakfast Smoothie

Ingredients:

- 1 banana
- 1 cup frozen berries (strawberries, blueberries, raspberries)
- 1 cup unsweetened almond milk
- 1 tbsp rolled oats
- 1 tsp honey (optional)

Instructions:

1. Peel and slice the banana.
2. In a blender, add the banana, frozen berries, almond milk, rolled oats, and honey (if using).
3. Blend until smooth.
4. Pour into a glass and enjoy your low-calorie breakfast smoothie. You can garnish with fresh berries or a sprinkle of rolled oats.
5. Enjoy!

Note: You can also add or substitute other ingredients like spinach, chia seeds, or peanut butter for added nutrition and flavor.

Breakfast Tacos

Ingredients:

- 2 corn tortillas
- 2 eggs
- 1/4 cup diced tomatoes
- 1/4 cup diced avocado
- 1/4 cup diced onion
- 1/4 cup diced bell pepper
- Salt and pepper to taste
- 1 tablespoon olive oil
- 1/4 cup shredded cheddar cheese
- Fresh cilantro for garnish

Instructions:

1. Heat a skillet over medium heat and add the olive oil.
2. Crack the eggs into the skillet and season with salt and pepper. Cook the eggs to your desired level of doneness.

3. While the eggs are cooking, add the diced tomatoes, avocado, onion, and bell pepper to a small bowl and mix together.

4. Once the eggs are done, place them on top of the tortillas.

5. Add the tomato mixture on top of the eggs.

6. Sprinkle shredded cheese over the top of the tacos.

7. Garnish with fresh cilantro.

8. Fold the tacos in half and enjoy!

Note: You can also use a low-calorie cheese or add more veggies to make it more healthy.

Breakfast Parfait

Ingredients:

- 1 cup plain Greek yogurt
- 1/4 cup rolled oats
- 1/4 cup mixed berries (such as blueberries, raspberries, and blackberries)
- 1 tbsp honey

- 1 tbsp chopped nuts (such as almonds or walnuts)

Instructions:

1. In a small bowl, mix together the Greek yogurt, rolled oats, and honey.
2. In a separate bowl, mix together the mixed berries.
3. In a glass or jar, layer the yogurt mixture, berry mixture, and chopped nuts. Repeat the layering until all ingredients have been used.
4. Serve and enjoy!

This breakfast parfait is a delicious and healthy way to start your day. The Greek yogurt provides protein and probiotics, while the oats and berries provide fiber and antioxidants. The honey and nuts add a touch of natural sweetness and crunch.

Low-Calorie Breakfast Smoothie

Ingredients:

- 1 banana
- 1 cup frozen berries (strawberries, blueberries, raspberries)
- 1/2 cup plain Greek yogurt
- 1/2 cup unsweetened almond milk
- 1 tsp honey (optional)
- 1 tsp chia seeds

Instructions:

1. In a blender, combine the banana, frozen berries, Greek yogurt, almond milk, honey (if using), and chia seeds.
2. Blend on high until smooth and creamy.
3. Pour into a glass and enjoy!

This smoothie is a great way to start your day with a boost of vitamins and antioxidants from the berries, protein from the yogurt and chia seeds, and a touch of sweetness from the banana and honey. The almond milk helps to keep the calorie count low, but you can use any other milk you prefer. It's a perfect balance of taste and health, satisfying your hunger without weighing you down. It's easy to prepare and you can enjoy it on the go, perfect for busy mornings.

Breakfast Omelette

Ingredients:

- 1 egg
- 1 egg white
- 1/4 cup diced bell pepper
- 1/4 cup diced onion
- 1/4 cup diced mushrooms
- Salt and pepper to taste
- 1 tsp olive oil

Instructions:

1. In a mixing bowl, whisk together the egg and egg white.
2. Heat a non-stick skillet over medium heat and add the olive oil.

3. Add the bell pepper, onion, and mushrooms to the skillet and sauté for 3-5 minutes until they are slightly softened.
4. Pour the egg mixture into the skillet and let it cook for 1-2 minutes, until the edges start to set.
5. Use a spatula to fold the omelette in half, and let it cook for an additional minute on each side.
6. Season with salt and pepper to taste and serve immediately.

This omelette is a great low-calorie option for breakfast. It's packed with vegetables and protein to keep you full and satisfied. Enjoy!

Side Dishes

Roasted Brussels Sprouts

Ingredients:

- 1 pound Brussels sprouts, trimmed and halved
- 2 tbsp olive oil
- Salt and pepper, to taste
- 1 tsp minced garlic
- 1 tsp grated Parmesan cheese (optional)

Instructions:

1. Preheat the oven to 400 degrees F (200 degrees C).
2. In a large bowl, toss the Brussels sprouts with olive oil, salt, pepper, and minced garlic.
3. Spread the Brussels sprouts in a single layer on a baking sheet.
4. Roast in the oven for 25-30 minutes, or until golden brown and tender.
5. Remove from the oven and sprinkle with grated Parmesan cheese (if desired).

6. Serve as a side dish or enjoy as a healthy snack.

Note: You can also add some lemon zest or a squeeze of lemon juice before roasting for added flavor.

Baked Eggplant

Ingredients:

- 1 medium eggplant, sliced
- 2 tbsp olive oil
- Salt and pepper, to taste
- 1 tsp dried oregano
- 1 tsp grated parmesan cheese (optional)

Instructions:

1. Preheat the oven to 375 degrees F (190 degrees C).
2. In a small bowl, mix together the olive oil, salt, pepper, and dried oregano to make a marinade.
3. Place the eggplant slices in a shallow dish and pour the marinade over them, making sure to coat each slice evenly.

4. Arrange the eggplant slices on a baking sheet and bake in the oven for 20-25 minutes or until tender and golden brown.

5. Remove from the oven and sprinkle with grated parmesan cheese (if desired).

6. Serve as a side dish or enjoy as a healthy snack.

Note: You can also add some balsamic vinegar or a squeeze of lemon juice before serving for added flavor.

Spicy Cauliflower

Ingredients:

- 1 head of cauliflower, cut into small florets
- 2 tbsp olive oil
- Salt and pepper, to taste
- 1 tsp cayenne pepper
- 1 tsp smoked paprika
- 1 tsp fresh lime juice

Instructions:

1. Preheat the oven to 425 degrees F (220 degrees C).

2. In a large bowl, toss the cauliflower florets with olive oil, salt, pepper, cayenne pepper, and smoked paprika.

3. Spread the cauliflower florets on a baking sheet and bake in the oven for 20-25 minutes, or until tender and golden brown.

4. Remove from the oven and squeeze fresh lime juice over the cauliflower.

5. Serve as a side dish or enjoy as a healthy snack.

Note: You can also add some chopped fresh cilantro for added flavor.

Steamed Asparagus

Ingredients:

- 1 bunch of asparagus
- 2 tbsp olive oil
- Salt and pepper, to taste
- 1 tsp lemon zest
- 1 tsp fresh lemon juice

Instructions:

1. Rinse the asparagus and trim off the woody ends.
2. Fill a large pot or pan with water and bring it to a boil.
3. Place the asparagus in a steamer basket or colander and lower it into the pot.
4. Cover and steam for about 4-6 minutes or until tender.
5. Remove from heat and toss with olive oil, salt, pepper, lemon zest, and lemon juice.
6. Serve as a side dish or enjoy as a healthy snack.

Note: You can also add some grated Parmesan cheese or chopped nuts for added flavor.

Grilled Zucchini

Ingredients:

- 2 medium zucchinis, sliced lengthwise
- 2 tbsp olive oil
- Salt and pepper, to taste
- 1 tsp dried basil
- 1 tsp fresh lemon juice

Instructions:

1. Preheat the grill to medium-high heat.
2. In a large bowl, toss the zucchini slices with olive oil, salt, pepper, and dried basil.
3. Grill the zucchini slices for about 2-3 minutes on each side, or until tender and slightly charred.
4. Remove from grill and squeeze fresh lemon juice over the zucchini.
5. Serve as a side dish or enjoy as a healthy snack.

Note: You can also add some grated Parmesan cheese or chopped fresh herbs for added flavor.

Roasted Brussels Sprouts with Thyme

Ingredients:

- 1 lb Brussels sprouts, trimmed and halved
- 2 tbsp olive oil
- Salt and pepper, to taste
- 1 tsp dried thyme
- 1 tsp balsamic vinegar

Instructions:

1. Preheat the oven to 425 degrees F (220 degrees C).
2. In a large bowl, toss the Brussels sprouts with olive oil, salt, pepper, and dried thyme.
3. Spread the Brussels sprouts on a baking sheet and roast in the oven for 25-30 minutes or until tender and golden brown.
4. Remove from the oven and drizzle with balsamic vinegar.
5. Serve as a side dish or enjoy as a healthy snack.

Note: You can also add some chopped nuts or grated Parmesan cheese for added flavor.

Roasted Eggplant

Ingredients:

- 1 medium eggplant, sliced into rounds
- 2 tbsp olive oil
- Salt and pepper, to taste
- 1 tsp garlic powder
- 1 tsp fresh chopped parsley

Instructions:

1. Preheat the oven to 400 degrees F (200 degrees C).
2. In a large bowl, toss the eggplant slices with olive oil, salt, pepper and garlic powder.
3. Spread the eggplant slices on a baking sheet and roast in the oven for 20-25 minutes or until tender and golden brown.
4. Remove from the oven and sprinkle with fresh chopped parsley.
5. Serve as a side dish or enjoy as a healthy snack.

Note: You can also add some grated Parmesan cheese or chopped fresh herbs for added flavor.

Cucumber, Lime and Tomato Salad

Ingredients:

- 2 medium cucumbers, sliced
- 2 medium tomatoes, diced
- 2 tbsp red onion, finely chopped
- 2 tbsp fresh lime juice
- 1 tbsp olive oil
- Salt and pepper, to taste
- 1 tsp fresh chopped cilantro

Instructions:

1. n a large bowl, mix together the cucumbers, tomatoes, red onion, lime juice, olive oil, salt and pepper.
2. Stir in the fresh cilantro and toss to combine.
3. Cover and refrigerate for at least 30 minutes to allow the flavors to meld.
4. Serve chilled as a side dish or enjoy as a healthy snack.

Note: You can also add some diced avocado or feta cheese for added flavor.

Grilled Asparagus

Ingredients:

- 1 lb asparagus, trimmed
- 2 tbsp olive oil
- Salt and pepper, to taste
- 1 tsp garlic powder
- 1 tbsp grated Parmesan cheese

Instructions:

1. Preheat the grill to medium-high heat.
2. In a large bowl, toss the asparagus with olive oil, salt, pepper, and garlic powder.
3. Grill the asparagus for about 2-3 minutes on each side or until tender and slightly charred.
4. Remove from grill and sprinkle with grated Parmesan cheese.
5. Serve as a side dish or enjoy as a healthy snack.

Note: You can also add some chopped fresh herbs for added flavor.

Main Dishes

Lemon Chicken with Asparagus

Ingredients:

- 4 boneless, skinless chicken breasts
- Salt and pepper, to taste
- 2 tbsp olive oil
- 1 tbsp fresh lemon juice
- 1 tsp dried oregano
- 1 lb asparagus, trimmed

Instructions:

1. Preheat the oven to 375 degrees F (190 degrees C).
2. Season the chicken breasts with salt and pepper.
3. In a small bowl, mix together olive oil, lemon juice, and oregano.
4. Place the chicken in a baking dish and brush with the lemon mixture.
5. Roast the chicken in the oven for 25-30 minutes or until cooked through.

6. While the chicken is cooking, in a separate pan sauté the asparagus in some oil for about 5-7 minutes or until tender.

7. Serve the chicken with the asparagus as a side dish.

Note: You can also add some chopped garlic or grated Parmesan cheese for added flavor.

Vegetable Stir Fry with Tofu

Ingredients:

- 1 block firm tofu, pressed and diced
- 2 tbsp oil (canola, vegetable or peanut)
- 1 red bell pepper, sliced
- 1 yellow bell pepper, sliced
- 1/2 cup sliced mushrooms
- 2 cloves garlic, minced
- 1/2 cup frozen peas
- 2 tbsp soy sauce
- 1 tbsp rice vinegar
- 1 tsp corn starch

- 1 tsp sesame oil
- Salt and pepper, to taste

Instructions:

1. In a large pan or wok, heat the oil over high heat.
2. Add the diced tofu and stir-fry for 5-7 minutes or until golden brown.
3. Remove the tofu from the pan and set aside.
4. In the same pan, add the red and yellow bell peppers, mushrooms, and garlic. Stir-fry for 2-3 minutes.
5. Add the frozen peas and stir-fry for another minute.
6. In a small bowl, mix together the soy sauce, rice vinegar, corn starch, sesame oil, salt and pepper.
7. Pour the sauce over the vegetables and stir well to coat.
8. Cook for another 2-3 minutes or until the sauce thickens.
9. Add the tofu back into the pan and stir to combine.
10. Serve over cooked rice or quinoa as a main dish.

Note: You can also add some sliced red onion, green onion or grated ginger for added flavor.

Grilled Chicken with Quinoa and Vegetable Salad

Ingredients:

- 4 boneless, skinless chicken breasts
- Salt and pepper, to taste
- 1 cup quinoa
- 2 cups chicken broth
- 1 red bell pepper, diced
- 1 yellow bell pepper, diced
- 1/2 red onion, diced
- 1/4 cup chopped fresh cilantro
- 2 tablespoons olive oil
- 1 lime, juiced
- 1 clove garlic, minced

Instructions:

1. Season the chicken with salt and pepper. Grill the chicken over medium-high heat for 6-8 minutes per side, or until cooked through.
2. In a medium saucepan, bring the chicken broth to a boil. Add the quinoa and reduce heat to low. Cover and simmer for 18-20 minutes, or until the quinoa is tender.

3. In a large bowl, combine the red and yellow bell peppers, red onion, cilantro, olive oil, lime juice, garlic, and a pinch of salt.

4. Add the cooked quinoa and toss to combine.

5. Serve the chicken with the quinoa salad on the side.

This dish is a low-calorie, healthy and delicious meal. It's packed with protein and nutrients and is perfect for a light dinner.

Baked Tilapia with Asparagus and Lemon

Ingredients:

- 4 tilapia fillets
- Salt and pepper, to taste
- 1 lb asparagus, trimmed
- 2 tbsp olive oil
- 2 cloves of garlic, minced
- 1 lemon, zested and juiced
- 1/4 cup chopped fresh parsley

Instructions:

1. Preheat your oven to 400 degrees F (200 degrees C).
2. Season the tilapia fillets with salt and pepper.
3. In a baking dish, place the asparagus and tilapia fillets. Drizzle with olive oil, minced garlic, lemon juice and zest.
4. Bake in the preheated oven for 12-15 minutes or until the fish is cooked through and the asparagus is tender.
5. Remove from the oven and sprinkle with chopped parsley.
6. Serve with your favourite side dish.

This dish is low in calories and high in protein, making it a perfect option for a healthy dinner. The combination of lemon and garlic add a fresh and delicious flavour to the fish, while the asparagus provides a healthy dose of vitamins and minerals.

Spicy Black Bean and Sweet Potato Tacos

Ingredients:

- 1 medium sweet potato, peeled and diced
- 1 tbsp olive oil
- Salt and pepper, to taste
- 1 can black beans, drained and rinsed
- 1/2 tsp cumin
- 1/4 tsp smoked paprika
- 1/4 tsp cayenne pepper
- 8 corn tortillas
- 1/4 cup diced red onion
- 1/4 cup diced fresh cilantro
- 1 lime, cut into wedges

Instructions:

1. Preheat your oven to 400 degrees F (200 degrees C).
2. In a baking sheet, toss the diced sweet potato with olive oil, salt and pepper. Roast in the preheated oven for 20-25 minutes or until fork-tender.

3. In a small saucepan, heat the black beans with cumin, smoked paprika, and cayenne pepper. Cook for 5 minutes or until heated through.

4. Warm the tortillas in a dry skillet or on a griddle for about 30 seconds per side.

5. Fill each tortilla with sweet potato, black bean mixture, diced red onion and cilantro.

6. Serve with lime wedges on the side.

7. Zucchini Noodle and Shrimp Stir-fry

Grilled Chicken and Vegetable Skewers

Ingredients:

- 1 pound boneless, skinless chicken breast, cut into 1-inch cubes
- Salt and pepper, to taste
- 1 red bell pepper, cut into 1-inch squares
- 1 yellow bell pepper, cut into 1-inch squares
- 1 red onion, cut into 1-inch squares
- 2 tbsp olive oil
- 2 cloves of garlic, minced

- 1 tsp dried oregano

- 1 tsp dried thyme

- 1 lemon, juiced

Instructions:

1. Preheat your grill to medium-high heat.

2. Season the chicken cubes with salt and pepper.

3. In a large bowl, mix together the vegetables, olive oil, garlic, oregano, thyme, and lemon juice.

4. Thread the chicken and vegetables onto skewers, alternating between the two.

5. Grill the skewers for 8-10 minutes per side or until the chicken is cooked through and the vegetables are slightly charred.

6. Serve with your favorite side dish.

Cauliflower Fried Rice

Ingredients:

- 1 head of cauliflower, grated

- 2 tbsp olive oil

- 1 small onion, diced
- 2 cloves of garlic, minced
- 1 cup frozen peas
- 1 cup diced carrots
- 2 eggs, lightly beaten
- 2 tbsp soy sauce
- 2 tbsp rice vinegar
- 1/4 cup chopped scallions

Instructions:

1. In a large skillet, heat the olive oil over medium-high heat. Add the onion and garlic and sauté for 2-3 minutes or until they are softened.
2. Add the grated cauliflower, frozen peas, and diced carrots. Stir-fry for 5-7 minutes or until the vegetables are tender.
3. Push the vegetables to one side of the skillet and add the beaten eggs to the other side. Scramble the eggs for 1-2 minutes or until they are cooked through.
4. Mix the soy sauce and rice vinegar together in a small bowl. Pour the mixture into the skillet and toss everything together.

5. Garnish with chopped scallions and serve.

Both dishes are low in calories and healthy, they are perfect options for a lighter dinner. The Grilled Chicken and Vegetable Skewers are packed with protein and vitamins and the Cauliflower Fried Rice is a great alternative to traditional fried rice made with white rice.

Black Bean and Sweet Potato Tacos

Ingredients:

- 2 medium sweet potatoes, peeled and diced
- 1 tbsp olive oil
- Salt and pepper, to taste
- 1 onion, diced
- 2 cloves of garlic, minced
- 1 can of black beans, drained and rinsed
- 1 tsp ground cumin
- 1/4 tsp smoked paprika
- 1/4 tsp chili powder
- 8 corn tortillas

- 1/2 cup diced tomatoes
- 1/4 cup chopped fresh cilantro
- Lime wedges, for serving

Instructions:

1. Preheat the oven to 400F (200C).
2. In a large mixing bowl, toss the sweet potatoes with olive oil, salt, and pepper. Spread them out on a baking sheet and roast for 20-25 minutes or until tender and golden brown.
3. Heat a large skillet over medium heat. Add the onion and garlic and sauté for 2-3 minutes or until they are softened.
4. Add the black beans, cumin, smoked paprika, and chili powder to the skillet. Stir and cook for an additional 2-3 minutes.
5. Heat the tortillas in a dry skillet over medium heat for a few seconds on each side or until they are warm and pliable.
6. To assemble the tacos, fill each tortilla with a spoonful of the black bean and sweet potato mixture. Add diced tomatoes, cilantro, and a squeeze of lime juice.

Spaghetti Squash with Spinach and Feta

Ingredients:

- 1 large spaghetti squash, halved and seeded
- 1 tbsp olive oil
- Salt and pepper, to taste
- 2 cloves of garlic, minced
- 2 cups of spinach, chopped
- 1/4 cup crumbled feta cheese
- 2 tbsp chopped fresh parsley

Instructions:

1. Preheat the oven to 375F (190C).
2. Place the squash halves cut-side down on a baking sheet and roast for 30-40 minutes or until tender.
3. Heat a large skillet over medium heat. Add the olive oil, garlic, and spinach. Cook for 2-3 minutes or until the spinach is wilted.
4. Remove the spaghetti squash from the oven and use a fork to scrape out the flesh. It will separate into spaghetti-like strands.

5. Add the spaghetti squash to the skillet with the spinach and toss to combine.

6. Remove from heat and add the crumbled feta cheese and parsley.

Both dishes are low in calories and healthy, they are perfect options for a lighter dinner. The Black Bean and Sweet Potato Tacos are a flavorful and satisfying option for vegetarians, and the Spaghetti Squash with Spinach and Feta is a tasty and low-carb alternative to traditional spaghetti.

Grilled Chicken with Zucchini Noodles and Pesto

Ingredients:

- 2 boneless, skinless chicken breasts
- Salt and pepper, to taste
- 2 zucchini, spiralized
- 2 tbsp basil pesto
- 2 tbsp grated Parmesan cheese

Instructions:

1. Preheat a grill to medium-high heat. Season the chicken breasts with salt and pepper.
2. Grill the chicken for 6-8 minutes per side or until cooked through.
3. In a large mixing bowl, toss the zucchini noodles with the pesto.
4. Serve the grilled chicken with the zucchini noodles and top with grated Parmesan cheese.

Quinoa and Black Bean Stuffed Peppers

Ingredients:

- 4 bell peppers, halved and seeded
- 1 cup cooked quinoa
- 1 can of black beans, drained and rinsed
- 1/2 cup diced tomatoes
- 1/4 cup diced onions
- 1 clove of garlic, minced
- 1/2 tsp cumin

- Salt and pepper, to taste
- 1/4 cup shredded cheddar cheese

Instructions:

1. Preheat the oven to 375F (190C).
2. In a large mixing bowl, combine the cooked quinoa, black beans, tomatoes, onions, garlic, cumin, salt, and pepper.
3. Stuff each pepper half with the quinoa mixture and place them in a baking dish.
4. Bake for 25-30 minutes or until the peppers are tender.
5. Sprinkle shredded cheddar cheese on top and return to the oven for an additional 5 minutes or until the cheese is melted.

Both of these dishes are low in calories and packed with flavor. The Grilled Chicken with Zucchini Noodles and Pesto is a healthy, low-carb alternative to pasta, and the Quinoa and Black Bean Stuffed Peppers is a satisfying and delicious vegetarian option.

Pan-Seared Tilapia with Tomato Caper Relish

Ingredients:

- 4 tilapia fillets
- Salt and pepper, to taste
- 2 tbsp olive oil
- 1 cup cherry tomatoes, halved
- 1/4 cup capers, drained
- 1/4 cup chopped fresh parsley
- 1/4 cup chopped fresh basil
- 2 cloves of garlic, minced
- 1 tbsp red wine vinegar
- 1 tbsp lemon juice

Instructions:

1. Season the tilapia fillets with salt and pepper.
2. In a large skillet, heat olive oil over medium-high heat.
3. Add the tilapia fillets to the skillet and cook for 3-4 minutes per side or until golden brown and cooked through.
4. Remove the tilapia fillets from the skillet and set aside.

5. In the same skillet, add the cherry tomatoes, capers, parsley, basil, garlic, red wine vinegar, and lemon juice. Cook for 2-3 minutes or until the tomatoes are softened.

6. Serve the tilapia fillets with the tomato caper relish on top.

Grilled Vegetable Skewers with Lemon Herb Vinaigrette

Ingredients:

- 2 large bell peppers, cut into chunks
- 1 large red onion, cut into chunks
- 2 cups cherry tomatoes
- 2 tbsp olive oil
- Salt and pepper, to taste
- 1/4 cup lemon juice
- 2 cloves of garlic, minced
- 2 tbsp chopped fresh parsley
- 2 tbsp chopped fresh basil

Instructions:

1. Preheat a grill to medium-high heat.
2. In a large bowl, toss the bell peppers, red onion, cherry tomatoes, olive oil, salt, and pepper.
3. Thread the vegetables onto skewers and grill for 8-10 minutes or until tender and slightly charred.
4. In a small bowl, mix together the lemon juice, garlic, parsley, and basil to make the vinaigrette.
5. Serve the grilled vegetable skewers with the lemon herb vinaigrette on the side.

Both of these dishes are low in calories and packed with flavor. The Pan-Seared Tilapia with Tomato Caper Relish is a light and fresh fish dish, and the Grilled Vegetable Skewers with Lemon Herb Vinaigrette is a satisfying and delicious vegetarian option.

Chicken and Zucchini Stir-Fry

Ingredients:

- 1 lb boneless, skinless chicken breast, cut into thin strips
- 2 zucchinis, cut into thin slices

- 1 red bell pepper, cut into thin strips
- 1 onion, thinly sliced
- 2 cloves of garlic, minced
- 2 tbsp sesame oil
- 2 tbsp soy sauce
- 1 tbsp rice vinegar
- 1 tsp grated ginger
- Salt and pepper, to taste
- Sesame seeds and chopped green onions for garnish

Instructions:

1. In a small bowl, mix together the soy sauce, rice vinegar, ginger, and a pinch of salt and pepper. Set aside.
2. Heat sesame oil in a large skillet or wok over high heat. Add the chicken and stir-fry for 3-4 minutes or until cooked through.
3. Remove the chicken from the skillet and set aside.
4. Add the zucchinis, red bell pepper, onion and garlic to the skillet and stir-fry for 2-3 minutes or until tender.
5. Return the chicken to the skillet and add the sauce. Stir-fry for another 1-2 minutes or until the sauce is thickened and the vegetables are coated.

6. Garnish with sesame seeds and chopped green onions

Spicy Quinoa and Black Bean Stuffed Peppers

Ingredients:

- 4 bell peppers
- 1 cup quinoa
- 2 cups vegetable broth
- 1 can black beans, drained and rinsed
- 1/2 red onion, diced
- 1 jalapeño pepper, seeded and diced
- 1/2 cup corn kernels
- 1/4 cup chopped cilantro
- 2 cloves of garlic, minced
- 1 tsp cumin
- Salt and pepper, to taste
- 1/2 cup shredded Monterey Jack cheese

Instructions:

1. Preheat the oven to 375°F (190°C).

2. Cut the tops off the bell peppers and remove the seeds and membranes.

3. Cook the quinoa according to package instructions using vegetable broth.

4. In a large bowl, mix together the cooked quinoa, black beans, red onion, jalapeño, corn, cilantro, garlic, cumin, and salt and pepper.

5. Stuff the quinoa mixture into the bell peppers, filling them to the top.

6. Place the peppers in a baking dish and bake for 20-25 minutes.

7. Remove from the oven and top each pepper with shredded cheese.

8. Bake for an additional 5-10 minutes or until the cheese is melted and bubbly.

Vegetarian Recipes

Vegetable and Tofu Curry

Ingredients:

- 1 block firm tofu, drained and cut into cubes
- 1 onion, chopped
- 2 cloves of garlic, minced
- 1 tbsp ginger, grated
- 1 tbsp curry powder
- 1 tsp cumin
- 1/4 tsp cayenne pepper
- 1 can of coconut milk
- 1 cup vegetable broth
- 1 cup diced carrots
- 1 cup diced potatoes
- 1 cup diced bell peppers
- 1 cup diced eggplant
- Salt and pepper, to taste
- Fresh cilantro for garnish

Instructions:

1. In a large pot or Dutch oven, heat a small amount of oil over medium heat. Add the onion, garlic and ginger and cook until softened, about 3 minutes.
2. Stir in the curry powder, cumin and cayenne pepper and cook for an additional 1 minute.
3. Add the vegetables, and cook for 5-7 minutes or until they start to soften.
4. Pour in the coconut milk and vegetable broth, and bring to a simmer.
5. Add the tofu and cook for an additional 10 minutes or until the vegetables are tender and the curry is heated through.
6. Season with salt and pepper, to taste.
7. Serve with rice and garnish with fresh cilantro.

Spinach and Feta Stuffed Portobello Mushrooms

Ingredients:

- 4 large portobello mushroom caps
- 1 tbsp olive oil
- 1/2 onion, diced
- 2 cloves of garlic, minced
- 1 cup spinach, chopped
- 1/4 cup feta cheese, crumbled
- 1/4 cup breadcrumbs
- Salt and pepper, to taste
- Optional: fresh herbs such as parsley or basil for garnish

Instructions:

1. Preheat the oven to 375°F (190°C).
2. Carefully remove the stems from the mushroom caps and scoop out the gills using a spoon.
3. Heat olive oil in a pan over medium heat. Add the onion and garlic and cook until softened, about 3 minutes.
4. Stir in the spinach and cook until wilted, about 2 minutes.

5. Remove from heat and stir in the feta cheese, breadcrumbs, and salt and pepper.

6. Stuff the mushroom caps with the spinach mixture.

7. Place the mushrooms on a baking sheet and bake for 20-25 minutes, or until the mushrooms are tender and the filling is hot and bubbly.

8. Garnish with fresh herbs, if desired.

Both of these dishes are low in calories and full of flavor, perfect for a healthy meal. The Vegetable and Tofu Curry is a comforting and delicious dish that is easy to customize to your own taste. The Spinach and Feta Stuffed Portobello Mushrooms is a satisfying and easy to make dish that is packed with nutrients, perfect for a light lunch or dinner.

Low-Calorie Quinoa and Vegetable Stir-Fry

Ingredients:

- 1 cup uncooked quinoa
- 1 cup sliced bell peppers
- 1 cup sliced mushrooms
- 1 cup sliced carrots

- 1 cup sliced onions

- 2 cloves of garlic, minced

- 1 tablespoon olive oil

- 2 tablespoons soy sauce

- Salt and pepper to taste

Instructions:

1. Cook quinoa according to package instructions.

2. In a pan, heat olive oil over medium heat. Add garlic and stir for about 30 seconds.

3. Add sliced vegetables and stir-fry for about 5-7 minutes or until vegetables are tender.

4. Add cooked quinoa, soy sauce, salt, and pepper to the pan and stir to combine.

5. Serve hot.

6.

Cucumber, Mint and Tomato Salad

Ingredients:

- 2 medium cucumbers, sliced

- 2 cups cherry tomatoes, halved

- 1/4 cup chopped fresh parsley
- 1/4 cup chopped fresh mint
- 2 tablespoons olive oil
- 2 tablespoons lemon juice
- Salt and pepper to taste

Instructions:

1. In a bowl, combine sliced cucumbers, cherry tomatoes, parsley and mint.
2. In a small separate bowl, mix olive oil, lemon juice, salt and pepper.
3. Pour the dressing over the salad and toss to combine.
4. Serve chilled.

Eggplant and Lentil Curry

Ingredients:

- 1 large eggplant, cubed
- 1 cup cooked lentils
- 1 onion, diced
- 2 cloves of garlic, minced

- 1 tablespoon curry powder
- 1/2 teaspoon ground cumin
- 1/2 teaspoon ground turmeric
- 1/2 teaspoon ground ginger
- 1/2 teaspoon ground coriander
- 1/2 teaspoon ground cinnamon
- 1 cup diced tomatoes
- 1 cup coconut milk
- Salt and pepper to taste

Instructions:

1. In a large pot, sauté onion and garlic in a little bit of oil until softened.
2. Add curry powder, cumin, turmeric, ginger, coriander and cinnamon and cook for 1-2 minutes more.
3. Add diced tomatoes, coconut milk and eggplant, bring to a simmer and cook for 15-20 minutes or until eggplant is soft.
4. Add cooked lentils, salt and pepper and cook for a few more minutes.
5. Serve over rice or with naan bread.

Broccoli and Tofu Stir-Fry

Ingredients:

- 1 cup broccoli florets
- 1 cup diced tofu
- 1/4 cup diced onions
- 1/4 cup diced bell peppers
- 1 tablespoon olive oil
- 2 tablespoons soy sauce
- 1 tablespoon rice vinegar
- 1 tablespoon honey
- Salt and pepper to taste

Instructions:

1. In a pan, heat olive oil over medium heat. Add diced onions, bell peppers, and broccoli and stir-fry for about 5-7 minutes or until vegetables are tender.
2. Add diced tofu and stir-fry for another 2-3 minutes.
3. In a small bowl, mix soy sauce, rice vinegar, and honey.
4. Pour the sauce over the stir-fry and toss to combine.

5. Serve hot.

Sweet Potato and Black Bean Enchiladas

Ingredients:

- 2 medium sweet potatoes, peeled and diced
- 1 can black beans, drained and rinsed
- 1/2 cup frozen corn
- 1/4 cup diced onions
- 1/4 cup diced bell pepper
- 2 cloves of garlic, minced
- 1 teaspoon chili powder
- 1/2 teaspoon ground cumin
- Salt and pepper to taste
- 6-8 corn tortillas
- 1 cup enchilada sauce
- 1/4 cup shredded cheddar cheese

Instructions:

1. Preheat oven to 375°F (190°C).

2. In a pan, heat a little bit of oil over medium heat. Add diced onions, bell pepper, and garlic and sauté for 1-2 minutes.

3. Add diced sweet potatoes, black beans, corn, chili powder, cumin, salt and pepper and sauté for another 5-7 minutes or until sweet potatoes are tender.

4. Spread some enchilada sauce on each tortilla, fill with sweet potato mixture and roll up.

5. Place the enchiladas seam side down in a baking dish and pour the remaining enchilada sauce over the top.

6. Sprinkle shredded cheese over the enchiladas.

7. Bake for 20-25 minutes or until cheese is melted and bubbly.

8. Serve hot.

Zucchini Noodles with Avocado Pesto

Ingredients:

- 4 medium zucchinis
- 1 ripe avocado
- 1/4 cup fresh basil leaves

- 2 cloves of garlic

- 1/4 cup grated parmesan cheese

- 2 tablespoons lemon juice

- 1/4 cup olive oil

- Salt and pepper to taste

Instructions:

1. Spiralize the zucchinis or use a julienne peeler to create zucchini noodles.

2. In a food processor, combine avocado, basil, garlic, parmesan cheese, lemon juice, salt and pepper. Pulse until well combined.

3. Slowly drizzle in the olive oil while the food processor is running until the pesto is smooth.

4. Toss the zucchini noodles with the avocado pesto.

5. Serve cold or at room temperature.

Grilled Eggplant and Tomato Stack

Ingredients:

- 1 large eggplant, sliced

- 1 large tomato, sliced
- 1/4 cup grated mozzarella cheese
- 2 tablespoons olive oil
- 2 tablespoons balsamic vinegar
- 2 cloves of garlic, minced
- Salt and pepper to taste
- Fresh basil leaves for garnish

Instructions:

1. Preheat grill to medium-high heat.
2. In a small bowl, mix together olive oil, balsamic vinegar, garlic, salt and pepper.
3. Brush the eggplant and tomato slices with the marinade.
4. Grill the eggplant and tomato slices for 2-3 minutes per side or until tender.
5. To assemble, place a grilled eggplant slice on a plate, top with a grilled tomato slice and sprinkle with mozzarella cheese. Repeat layering until all slices are used.
6. Garnish with fresh basil leaves.
7. Serve hot.

Zucchini and Parmesan Fritters

Ingredients:

- 2 medium zucchinis, grated
- 1/4 cup all-purpose flour
- 2 tablespoons grated Parmesan cheese
- 1 egg
- Salt and pepper to taste
- 2 tablespoons olive oil

Instructions:

1. In a large bowl, mix together the zucchini, flour, Parmesan cheese, egg, salt and pepper.
2. In a large pan over medium heat, add the olive oil.
3. Using a spoon, drop spoonfuls of the zucchini mixture into the pan. Flatten the fritters with the back of the spoon.
4. Cook for 2-3 minutes per side or until golden brown.
5. Repeat with the remaining mixture.
6. Serve warm.

Lentil and Vegetable Soup

Ingredients:

- 1 tablespoon olive oil
- 1 onion, diced
- 2 cloves of garlic, minced
- 2 cups diced mixed vegetables (such as carrots, celery, and bell peppers)
- 1 cup green or brown lentils, rinsed and drained
- 4 cups vegetable broth
- 1 teaspoon dried thyme
- Salt and pepper to taste
- Optional toppings: diced tomatoes, chopped parsley

Instructions:

1. In a large pot over medium heat, add the olive oil and sauté the onion and garlic for 2-3 minutes or until softened.
2. Add the mixed vegetables and cook for an additional 5-7 minutes or until the vegetables are tender.

3. Stir in the lentils, vegetable broth, and thyme. Bring to a boil, then reduce the heat and simmer for 25-30 minutes or until the lentils are tender.

4. Season with salt and pepper to taste.

5. Garnish with diced tomatoes and chopped parsley if desired.

Cucumber and Avocado Salad

Ingredients:

- 2 large cucumbers, peeled and diced
- 1 large avocado, peeled and diced
- 1/4 cup diced red onion
- 2 tablespoons chopped fresh cilantro
- 2 tablespoons lime juice
- 1 tablespoon olive oil
- Salt and pepper to taste

Instructions:

1. In a large bowl, combine the cucumbers, avocado, red onion and cilantro.

2. In a small bowl, whisk together the lime juice, olive oil, salt and pepper.

3. Pour the dressing over the salad and toss to coat well.

4. Let sit for at least 15 minutes to let the flavors meld together.

5. Taste and adjust seasoning as necessary.

Quinoa and Black Bean Salad

Ingredients:

- 1 cup quinoa, rinsed and drained
- 1 1/2 cups water
- 1 can black beans, rinsed and drained
- 1/2 red bell pepper, diced
- 1/2 red onion, diced
- 1 jalapeno pepper, seeded and diced
- 2 cloves of garlic, minced
- 2 tablespoons chopped fresh cilantro
- 2 tablespoons lime juice
- 1 tablespoon olive oil
- Salt and pepper to taste

Instructions:

1. In a medium saucepan, bring the quinoa and water to a boil. Reduce heat and simmer, covered, for 15-20 minutes or until the quinoa is tender and the water has been absorbed.
2. Fluff with a fork and let cool.
3. In a large bowl, combine the cooked quinoa, black beans, red bell pepper, red onion, jalapeno pepper and garlic.
4. In a small bowl, whisk together the lime juice, olive oil, salt and pepper.
5. Pour the dressing over the salad and toss to coat well.
6. Stir in cilantro.
7. Taste and adjust seasoning as necessary.
8. Can be served cold or at room temperature

Roasted Eggplant and Tomato Salad

Ingredients:

- 2 medium eggplants, cut into cubes
- 1 pint cherry tomatoes, halved
- 2 cloves of garlic, minced
- 2 tablespoons olive oil
- Salt and pepper to taste
- 1/4 cup chopped fresh basil

Instructions:

1. Preheat oven to 375°F (190°C).
2. In a large bowl, toss the eggplant cubes, cherry tomatoes, garlic, olive oil, salt, and pepper together.
3. Spread the mixture out on a baking sheet in a single layer.
4. Roast for 20-25 minutes or until the eggplant is tender and the tomatoes are slightly browned.
5. Remove from the oven and let cool.
6. Once cooled, add the chopped basil and toss to combine.
7. Serve at room temperature or chilled.

Grilled Zucchini and Bell Pepper Salad

Ingredients:

- 2 medium zucchinis, sliced
- 2 bell peppers (red and yellow), sliced
- 2 cloves of garlic, minced
- 2 tablespoons olive oil
- Salt and pepper to taste
- 2 tablespoons lemon juice
- 1/4 cup chopped fresh parsley

Instructions:

1. Preheat grill to medium-high heat.
2. In a large bowl, toss the zucchini slices, bell pepper slices, garlic, olive oil, salt, and pepper together.
3. Grill the vegetables for 6-8 minutes per side or until they are slightly charred and tender.
4. Remove from the grill and let cool.
5. Once cooled, add the lemon juice and chopped parsley and toss to combine.
6. Serve at room temperature or chilled.

Fish Recipes

Baked Cod with Lemon and Garlic

Ingredients:

- 4 cod fillets
- 2 tbsp olive oil
- 2 cloves of garlic, minced
- 1 lemon, juiced and zested
- Salt and pepper to taste
- Fresh parsley, chopped (for garnish)

Instructions:

1. Preheat your oven to 400 degrees F.
2. In a small bowl, mix together olive oil, minced garlic, lemon juice, and lemon zest. Season with salt and pepper to taste.
3. Place cod fillets in a baking dish and pour the lemon and garlic mixture over the fish.

4. Bake in the oven for 12-15 minutes, or until the fish is cooked through and flakes easily.

5. Garnish with fresh parsley before serving.

Grilled Salmon with Pineapple Salsa

Ingredients:

- 4 salmon fillets
- 2 tbsp olive oil
- Salt and pepper to taste
- 1 cup diced pineapple
- 1/4 cup diced red onion
- 1/4 cup diced red bell pepper
- 1 tbsp chopped cilantro
- 1 tbsp lime juice

Instructions:

1. Preheat your grill to medium-high heat.
2. Brush salmon fillets with olive oil and season with salt and pepper.

3. Grill the salmon for about 4-5 minutes per side, or until cooked through.

4. In a small bowl, mix together diced pineapple, red onion, red bell pepper, cilantro, and lime juice.

5. Serve the grilled salmon with the pineapple salsa on top.

Pan-Seared Tilapia with Spinach and Tomatoes

Ingredients:

- 4 tilapia fillets
- 2 tbsp olive oil
- 2 cloves of garlic, minced
- 1/2 tsp paprika
- Salt and pepper to taste
- 1 cup baby spinach
- 1/2 cup cherry tomatoes, halved
- 1 tbsp lemon juice

Instructions:

1. Heat olive oil in a large skillet over medium heat. Add minced garlic and paprika, and cook for 1-2 minutes until fragrant.
2. Season tilapia fillets with salt and pepper, and add them to the skillet. Cook for 3-4 minutes per side, or until the fish is cooked through and flaky.
3. Remove the tilapia from the skillet and set aside.
4. In the same skillet, add baby spinach and cherry tomatoes. Cook until the spinach has wilted and the tomatoes are softened.
5. Stir in lemon juice and cook for an additional minute.
6. Serve the tilapia fillets with the spinach and tomato mixture on top.

Lemon and Herb-Crusted Mahi Mahi

Ingredients:

- 4 Mahi Mahi fillets
- 2 tbsp olive oil

- 1 tbsp lemon juice
- 1 tsp Dijon mustard
- 1/4 cup breadcrumbs
- 2 tbsp chopped fresh parsley
- 2 tbsp chopped fresh basil
- Salt and pepper to taste

Instructions:

1. Preheat the oven to 400 degrees F.
2. In a small bowl, mix together olive oil, lemon juice, and Dijon mustard.
3. In another bowl, mix together breadcrumbs, parsley, basil, and a pinch of salt and pepper.
4. Brush the Mahi Mahi fillets with the olive oil mixture, then press the breadcrumb mixture onto the fish, coating it evenly.
5. Place the fish on a baking sheet lined with parchment paper and bake for 12-15 minutes, or until the fish is cooked through and the crust is golden brown.
6. Serve hot and enjoy!

Steamed Halibut with Ginger and Scallions

Ingredients:

- 4 halibut fillets
- 2 tbsp soy sauce
- 1 tbsp rice vinegar
- 1 tbsp honey
- 1 tsp grated ginger
- 2 cloves of garlic, minced
- 2 scallions, sliced
- Salt and pepper to taste

Instructions:

1. In a small bowl, mix together soy sauce, rice vinegar, honey, grated ginger, minced garlic, scallions and a pinch of salt and pepper.
2. Place the halibut fillets in a heatproof dish, and pour the marinade over the fish.
3. Cover the dish with foil and steam it over high heat for 8-10 minutes, or until the fish is cooked through and flaky.

4. Serve the steamed halibut with the marinade sauce poured on top.

Baked Barramundi with Tomato and Zucchini

Ingredients:

- 4 barramundi fillets
- 2 tbsp olive oil
- 1 tsp smoked paprika
- Salt and pepper to taste
- 1 small zucchini, sliced
- 1 cup cherry tomatoes, halved
- 1/4 cup chopped fresh basil
- 2 tbsp grated Parmesan cheese

Instructions:

1. Preheat the oven to 425 degrees F.
2. In a small bowl, mix together olive oil, smoked paprika and a pinch of salt and pepper.
3. Place the barramundi fillets in a baking dish and brush them with the olive oil mixture.

4. Arrange the sliced zucchini and halved cherry tomatoes around the fish.

5. Sprinkle with chopped basil and grated Parmesan cheese.

6. Bake for 12-15 minutes or until the fish is cooked through and the vegetables are tender.

7. Serve hot and enjoy!

Grilled Sardines with Lemon and Thyme

Ingredients:

- 8 sardines, cleaned and scaled
- 2 tbsp olive oil
- 2 cloves of garlic, minced
- 2 tbsp lemon juice
- 1 tsp dried thyme
- Salt and pepper to taste

Instructions:

1. In a small bowl, mix together olive oil, minced garlic, lemon juice, dried thyme and a pinch of salt and pepper.

2. Place the sardines in a shallow dish, and pour the marinade over the fish.

3. Marinate the sardines in the fridge for 30 minutes to an hour.

4. Preheat the grill to high heat.

5. Grill the sardines for 3-4 minutes per side, or until the fish is cooked through and flaky.

6. Serve the grilled sardines with lemon wedges and extra thyme sprigs on top.

Baked Cod with Fennel and Lemon

Ingredients:

- 4 cod fillets
- 2 tbsp olive oil
- 1 small fennel bulb, sliced
- 2 cloves of garlic, minced
- 2 tbsp lemon juice
- 1 tsp dried oregano
- Salt and pepper to taste

Instructions:

1. Preheat the oven to 375 degrees F.
2. In a small bowl, mix together olive oil, minced garlic, lemon juice, dried oregano and a pinch of salt and pepper.
3. Place the cod fillets in a baking dish and brush them with the olive oil mixture.
4. Arrange the sliced fennel around the fish.
5. Bake for 12-15 minutes or until the fish is cooked through and the vegetables are tender.
6. Serve hot and enjoy!

Poached Salmon with Asparagus and Lemon

Ingredients:

- 4 salmon fillets
- 2 cups chicken or vegetable broth
- 1/4 cup white wine
- 1 tbsp lemon juice

- 2 cloves of garlic, minced

- 1 bunch of asparagus, trimmed

- Salt and pepper to taste

Instructions:

1. In a large pot, bring the broth, white wine, lemon juice, minced garlic and a pinch of salt and pepper to a simmer.

2. Add the salmon fillets to the pot and reduce the heat to low. Cover and poach the fish for 8-10 minutes, or until the fish is cooked through and flaky.

3. Remove the salmon from the pot and place it on a plate.

4. Add the asparagus to the poaching liquid and cook for 2-3 minutes or until tender.

5. Drain the asparagus and place it around the salmon.

6. Serve the poached salmon with asparagus and the poaching liquid as a sauce.

Baked Tilapia with Spinach and Cream

Ingredients:

- 4 tilapia fillets
- 1 tbsp olive oil
- 2 cloves of garlic, minced
- 1/4 cup heavy cream
- 1/4 cup grated Parmesan cheese
- 2 cups fresh spinach
- Salt and pepper to taste

Instructions:

1. Preheat the oven to 400 degrees F.
2. In a pan, heat the olive oil and sauté the minced garlic for 1-2 minutes.
3. Add the heavy cream and grated Parmesan cheese, stir to combine.
4. Add the fresh spinach and cook until wilted.
5. Season the tilapia fillets with salt and pepper.
6. Place the fillets in a baking dish and top each one with the spinach mixture.

7. Bake for 12-15 minutes or until the fish is cooked through.

8. Serve hot and enjoy!

Lemon and Herb Baked Halibut

Ingredients:

- 4 halibut fillets
- 2 tbsp olive oil
- 2 tbsp lemon juice
- 1 tsp dried basil
- 1 tsp dried oregano
- 1 tsp dried thyme
- Salt and pepper to taste

Instructions:

1. Preheat the oven to 425 degrees F.

2. In a small bowl, mix together olive oil, lemon juice, dried basil, oregano, thyme, salt and pepper.

3. Place the halibut fillets in a baking dish and brush them with the lemon and herb mixture.

4. Bake the halibut for 12-15 minutes or until the fish is cooked through and flaky.

5. Serve the baked halibut with lemon wedges and extra herbs on top.

Pan-Seared Tilapia with Mango Salsa

Ingredients:

- 4 tilapia fillets
- 1 tbsp olive oil
- 1 ripe mango, peeled and diced
- 1/4 red onion, finely diced
- 1/4 red pepper, finely diced
- 2 tbsp lime juice
- 1 tsp honey
- Salt and pepper to taste

Instructions:

1. In a medium bowl, mix together diced mango, red onion, red pepper, lime juice, honey, salt and pepper.

2. Heat olive oil in a pan over medium-high heat.

3. Season the tilapia fillets with salt and pepper, and add them to the pan. Cook for 2-3 minutes per side or until the fish is cooked through.

4. Remove the fish from the pan, and serve it with the mango salsa on top.

5. Enjoy!

Grilled Sardines with Tomato and Olive Relish

Ingredients:

- 8 fresh sardines, cleaned and deboned
- 1 tbsp olive oil
- Salt and pepper to taste
- 2 ripe tomatoes, diced
- 1/4 cup of chopped kalamata olives
- 2 cloves of garlic, minced
- 1 tbsp red wine vinegar
- 1 tbsp chopped fresh parsley

Instructions:

1. Preheat the grill to medium-high heat.

2. Season the sardines with olive oil, salt and pepper.

3. Grill the sardines for 2-3 minutes per side, or until cooked through.

4. While the sardines are grilling, combine the tomatoes, olives, garlic, red wine vinegar, and parsley in a small bowl.

5. Serve the grilled sardines with the tomato and olive relish on top.

Pan-Seared Cod with Cilantro Lime Butter

Ingredients:

- 4 cod fillets
- 2 tbsp olive oil
- Salt and pepper to taste
- 1/4 cup unsalted butter
- 2 cloves of garlic, minced
- 2 tbsp lime juice
- 2 tbsp chopped fresh cilantro

Instructions:

1. Heat the olive oil in a pan over medium-high heat.

2. Season the cod fillets with salt and pepper, and add them
    to the pan. Cook for 2-3 minutes per side or until the
    fish is cooked through.

3. Remove the fish from the pan, and keep it warm.

4. In the same pan, melt the butter and add the minced
    garlic, lime juice and cilantro. Cook for 1-2 minutes.

5. Serve the cod fillets with the cilantro lime butter on top.

6. Enjoy!

Baked Salmon with Avocado Salsa

Ingredients:

- 4 salmon fillets
- 2 tbsp olive oil
- Salt and pepper to taste
- 1 ripe avocado, diced
- 1/4 red onion, diced
- 1/4 cup diced cilantro

- 2 tbsp lime juice
- 1 clove of garlic, minced

Instructions:

1. Preheat the oven to 425 degrees F.
2. Season the salmon fillets with olive oil, salt and pepper.
3. Place the salmon fillets in a baking dish and bake for 12-15 minutes or until the fish is cooked through and flaky.
4. While the salmon is baking, mix together diced avocado, red onion, cilantro, lime juice, and garlic in a small bowl.
5. Serve the baked salmon with avocado salsa on top.

Pan-Seared Sea Bass with Lemon Caper Butter

Ingredients:

- 4 sea bass fillets
- 2 tbsp olive oil
- Salt and pepper to taste
- 1/4 cup unsalted butter
- 2 tbsp capers, drained
- 2 tbsp lemon juice

- 1 clove of garlic, minced

Instructions:

1. Heat the olive oil in a pan over medium-high heat.
2. Season the sea bass fillets with salt and pepper, and add them to the pan. Cook for 2-3 minutes per side or until the fish is cooked through.
3. Remove the fish from the pan, and keep it warm.
4. In the same pan, melt the butter and add the capers, lemon juice, and minced garlic. Cook for 1-2 minutes.
5. Serve the sea bass fillets with the lemon caper butter on top.
6. Enjoy!

Desserts

Strawberry and Yogurt Parfait

Ingredients:

- 1 cup fresh strawberries, hulled and sliced
- 1 cup plain Greek yogurt
- 2 tablespoons honey
- 1 teaspoon vanilla extract
- 1/4 cup granola (optional)

Instructions:

1. In a small bowl, mix together the yogurt, honey, and vanilla extract.
2. Layer the strawberries and yogurt mixture in a glass or jar.
3. Repeat layers until all ingredients are used up.
4. Top with granola, if desired.
5. Serve immediately or store in the refrigerator for up to 2 hours before serving.

Chocolate Banana Ice Cream

Ingredients:

- 2 ripe bananas, peeled and frozen
- 2 tablespoons cocoa powder
- 1 teaspoon vanilla extract
- 1 tablespoon honey (optional)

Instructions:

1. Cut the frozen bananas into small chunks and place them in a food processor or blender.
2. Add the cocoa powder, vanilla extract, and honey (if using) to the food processor or blender.
3. Blend until the mixture is smooth and creamy, stopping to scrape down the sides of the container as needed.
4. Serve immediately or transfer to an airtight container and freeze for at least 2 hours before serving.
5. If the ice cream has hardened too much, let it sit at room temperature for a few minutes before scooping.

Blueberry Cheesecake Bites

Ingredients:

- 1 cup blueberries
- 1 cup low-fat cream cheese
- 1/4 cup granulated sugar
- 1 teaspoon vanilla extract
- 1/4 cup graham cracker crumbs

Instructions:

1. Preheat the oven to 350°F (175°C) and line a baking sheet with parchment paper.
2. In a medium bowl, mix together the cream cheese, sugar, and vanilla extract until smooth.
3. Fold in the blueberries and graham cracker crumbs.
4. Using a tablespoon, scoop out small portions of the mixture and shape them into bite-sized balls.
5. Place the bites on the prepared baking sheet and bake for 10-12 minutes, until lightly golden brown.
6. Allow the bites to cool before serving.

Chocolate Mousse

Ingredients:

- 1/2 cup dark chocolate chips
- 1/2 cup heavy cream
- 1/4 cup granulated sugar
- 2 egg whites

Instructions:

1. In a medium saucepan, heat the cream and sugar over medium heat until it comes to a simmer.
2. Remove from heat and add the chocolate chips, stirring until they are melted and the mixture is smooth.
3. In a separate bowl, beat the egg whites until stiff peaks form.
4. Gently fold the egg whites into the chocolate mixture.
5. Divide the mousse into small ramekins or glasses and refrigerate for at least 1 hour before serving.

Strawberry Yogurt Popsicles

Ingredients:

- 1 cup fresh strawberries
- 1 cup plain Greek yogurt
- 1/4 cup honey
- 1 teaspoon vanilla extract

1. Instructions:
2. In a blender or food processor, puree the strawberries until smooth.
3. Add the Greek yogurt, honey, and vanilla extract to the blender and pulse until well combined.
4. Pour the mixture into popsicle molds and freeze for at least 4 hours, or until frozen solid.
5. To remove the popsicles from the molds, run them under warm water for a few seconds before gently pulling the popsicles out.

Chocolate Banana Bites

Ingredients:

- 2 ripe bananas
- 1/2 cup dark chocolate chips
- 1/4 cup chopped nuts (optional)

Instructions:

1. Peel and slice the bananas into 1/2-inch rounds.
2. Melt the chocolate chips in a microwave-safe bowl or on a double boiler.
3. Dip each banana slice into the chocolate, using a fork to help coat it evenly.
4. Place the chocolate-coated banana slices on a baking sheet lined with parchment paper.
5. Sprinkle the chopped nuts on top of the banana slices, if desired.
6. Freeze the banana bites for at least 2 hours, or until the chocolate is fully hardened.
7. Remove the banana bites from the freezer and allow them to sit at room temperature for a few minutes before serving.

Mango Sorbet

Ingredients:

- 2 cups frozen mango chunks
- 1/4 cup agave nectar
- 1/4 cup freshly squeezed lime juice

Instructions:

1. In a blender or food processor, blend the frozen mango chunks until smooth.
2. Add the agave nectar and lime juice to the blender and pulse until well combined.
3. Taste the mixture and adjust the sweetness or acidity as desired.
4. Transfer the sorbet to an airtight container and freeze for at least 2 hours, or until firm.
5. Scoop the sorbet into bowls and serve immediately.

Chocolate Chia Pudding

Ingredients:

- 1 cup almond milk
- 1/4 cup chia seeds
- 2 tablespoons unsweetened cocoa powder
- 1 tablespoon honey or agave nectar
- 1 teaspoon vanilla extract
- Pinch of salt

Instructions:

1. In a medium mixing bowl, combine the almond milk, chia seeds, cocoa powder, honey or agave nectar, vanilla extract, and salt. Whisk until well combined.
2. Cover the bowl with plastic wrap and refrigerate for at least 2 hours or overnight.
3. Whisk the pudding again before serving to ensure that the chia seeds are evenly distributed.
4. Serve chilled, garnished with fresh berries or shredded coconut if desired.

Strawberry Yogurt Parfait

Ingredients:

- 1 cup fresh strawberries, hulled and diced
- 1/2 cup plain low-fat Greek yogurt
- 2 tablespoons honey
- 1/4 cup granola

Instructions:

1. In a small saucepan, cook the strawberries over medium heat until they release their juice and become soft. Mash the strawberries with a fork and set aside to cool.
2. In a small mixing bowl, mix the Greek yogurt and honey until well combined.
3. Layer the strawberry compote, yogurt mixture and granola in a glass or jar.
4. Repeat layering until all ingredients are used up.
5. Serve chilled and enjoy!

Strawberry Cheesecake

Ingredients:

- 8 oz light cream cheese, at room temperature
- 1/4 cup granulated sugar
- 1 tsp vanilla extract
- 1/2 cup low-fat Greek yogurt
- 2 eggs
- 1/2 cup fresh strawberries, diced
- 1/4 cup graham cracker crumbs
- 1 tbsp butter, melted

Instructions:

1. Preheat oven to 350F (175C).
2. In a large mixing bowl, beat cream cheese, sugar, and vanilla extract until smooth.
3. Mix in Greek yogurt and eggs, one at a time, until well combined.
4. Fold in diced strawberries and graham cracker crumbs.
5. Pour mixture into a 9-inch (23cm) springform pan that has been coated with melted butter.

6. Bake for 25-30 minutes, or until the edges are golden brown and the center is slightly jiggly.

7. Let cool to room temperature before refrigerating for at least 2 hours before serving.

Low-Calorie Blueberry Cheesecake

Ingredients:

- 8 oz light cream cheese, at room temperature
- 1/4 cup granulated sugar
- 1 tsp vanilla extract
- 1/2 cup low-fat Greek yogurt
- 2 eggs
- 1/2 cup fresh blueberries
- 1/4 cup graham cracker crumbs
- 1 tbsp butter, melted

Instructions:

1. Preheat oven to 350F (175C).
2. In a large mixing bowl, beat cream cheese, sugar, and vanilla extract until smooth.

3. Mix in Greek yogurt and eggs, one at a time, until well combined.

4. Fold in fresh blueberries and graham cracker crumbs.

5. Pour mixture into a 9-inch (23cm) springform pan that has been coated with melted butter.

6. Bake for 25-30 minutes, or until the edges are golden brown and the center is slightly jiggly.

7. Let cool to room temperature before refrigerating for at least 2 hours before serving.

Blueberry Oat Muffins

Ingredients:

- 1 cup rolled oats
- 1/2 cup almond milk
- 1/4 cup maple syrup
- 1 ripe banana
- 1 cup fresh blueberries
- 1 tsp baking powder
- 1/4 tsp salt
- 1 tsp vanilla extract

Instructions:

1. Preheat the oven to 375°F (190°C) and line a muffin tin with paper liners.
2. In a medium bowl, mix together the oats, almond milk, maple syrup, and mashed banana.
3. In a separate bowl, mix together the baking powder, salt, and blueberries.
4. Add the dry ingredients to the wet ingredients and stir until just combined.
5. Pour the batter into the prepared muffin tin, filling each cup about 2/3 full.
6. Bake for 18-20 minutes, or until a toothpick inserted into the center of a muffin comes out clean.
7. Let the muffins cool in the tin for 5 minutes before transferring them to a wire rack to cool completely.

Lemon Poppyseed Muffins

Ingredients:

- 1 cup all-purpose flour

- 1/2 cup granulated sugar
- 1 tsp baking powder
- 1/4 tsp salt
- 1/4 cup vegetable oil
- 1/4 cup plain yogurt
- 1 egg
- 1 tsp lemon zest
- 1 tbsp lemon juice
- 1 tsp poppyseeds

Instructions:

1. Preheat the oven to 375°F (190°C) and line a muffin tin with paper liners.
2. In a medium bowl, mix together the flour, sugar, baking powder, and salt.
3. In a separate bowl, mix together the vegetable oil, yogurt, egg, lemon zest, lemon juice and poppyseeds.
4. Add the wet ingredients to the dry ingredients and stir until just combined.
5. Pour the batter into the prepared muffin tin, filling each cup about 2/3 full.

6. Bake for 18-20 minutes, or until a toothpick inserted into the center of a muffin comes out clean.

7. Let the muffins cool in the tin for 5 minutes before transferring them to a wire rack to cool completely.

Chocolate & Avocado Mousse

Ingredients:

- 1 ripe avocado
- 1/4 cup unsweetened cocoa powder
- 1/4 cup almond milk
- 2 tbsp maple syrup
- 1 tsp vanilla extract
- Pinch of salt

Instructions:

1. In a food processor, combine the avocado, cocoa powder, almond milk, maple syrup, vanilla extract, and salt. Blend until smooth and creamy.

2. Divide the mousse into small bowls or cups.

3. Chill in the refrigerator for at least 30 minutes before serving

Berry Sorbet

Ingredients:

- 1 cup frozen mixed berries
- 1/4 cup almond milk
- 2 tbsp agave syrup
- 1 tsp lemon juice
- Pinch of salt

Instructions:

1. In a blender, combine the frozen mixed berries, almond milk, agave syrup, lemon juice, and salt. Blend until smooth.
2. Pour the mixture into a container and freeze for at least 2 hours.
3. Scoop the sorbet into bowls and serve.

Chocolate Chia Pudding

Ingredients:

- 1 cup unsweetened almond milk
- 1/4 cup chia seeds
- 2 tbsp unsweetened cocoa powder
- 1 tbsp maple syrup
- 1 tsp vanilla extract

Instructions:

1. In a medium mixing bowl, whisk together the almond milk, chia seeds, cocoa powder, maple syrup, and vanilla extract until well combined.
2. Cover the bowl with plastic wrap or a lid and refrigerate for at least 2 hours or overnight.
3. Once the pudding has thickened, give it a good stir.
4. Divide the pudding into two bowls or cups and enjoy!

Banana Oat Cookies

Ingredients:

- 1 ripe banana
- 1 cup rolled oats
- 1/4 cup sugar-free sweetener
- 1 tsp vanilla extract
- 1/4 tsp baking powder
- Pinch of salt
- Optional: 1/4 cup chocolate chips or nuts

Instructions:

1. Preheat the oven to 350°F (175°C) and line a baking sheet with parchment paper.
2. In a medium bowl, mash the banana until smooth.
3. Stir in the oats, sweetener, vanilla extract, baking powder, salt, and any optional ingredients.
4. Using a spoon or cookie scoop, drop dough onto the prepared baking sheet.
5. Bake for 12-15 minutes or until golden brown.
6. Let cool on the baking sheet for 5 minutes before transferring to a wire rack to cool completely

Exercises to do for a healthy life

It is important to do exercises for maintaining a healthy weight, losing weight, and overall health. Regular exercise helps to boost metabolism, burn calories and fat, and build muscle mass. It also improves cardiovascular health, strengthens bones, and reduces the risk of chronic diseases such as diabetes, heart disease, and certain cancers. Additionally, exercise has been shown to improve mood, reduce stress and anxiety, and promote better sleep. Overall, regular exercise is essential for maintaining a healthy and active lifestyle.

1. **Jumping Jacks:**

- Begin standing with your feet together and your arms at your sides.
- Jump your feet out to the sides and raise your arms above your head at the same time.
- Jump your feet back together and lower your arms.
- Repeat for 30 seconds to 1 minute.

2. Squats:

- Start with your feet shoulder-width apart, and your arms extended straight out in front of you.
- Bend your knees, pushing your hips back and lowering your body as if you were sitting back into a chair.
- Keep your weight in your heels and your knees behind your toes.
- Push back up to the starting position.
- Repeat for 30 seconds to 1 minute.

3. Plank:

- Begin on your hands and knees, with your hands shoulder-width apart and your knees hip-width apart.
- Walk your hands forward so that you are on your toes and your hands, with your body in a straight line from your head to your heels.
- Hold this position for 30 seconds to 1 minute.

4. Lunges:

- Start standing with your feet shoulder-width apart.
- Take a large step forward with one foot and lower your body until your thigh is parallel to the ground and your knee is directly over your ankle.
- Push back to the starting position and repeat with the opposite leg.
- Repeat for 30 seconds to 1 minute.

5. Bicycle Crunches:

- Lie on your back with your knees bent and your hands behind your head.
- Lift your shoulders off the ground and bring your right elbow towards your left knee.
- Straighten your right leg out as you twist to the opposite side and bring your left elbow towards your right knee.
- Repeat for 30 seconds to 1 minute.

Conclusion

In conclusion, this low-carb recipe book has provided a wide variety of delicious and healthy meal options for those looking to reduce their carbohydrate intake. From breakfast to dinner, and everything in between, these recipes are designed to help you reach your health and weight loss goals while still enjoying delicious and satisfying meals. Whether you're new to the low-carb lifestyle or a seasoned pro, these recipes are sure to become a staple in your kitchen. We hope you have enjoyed the journey and found something new and delicious to try, and we look forward to hearing about your culinary creations. Remember that, even though you are following a low-carb diet, it's important to eat a balanced, healthy diet and to get enough of the right types of carbs. Happy cooking!

9 788367 110563